This book is dedicated to my husband, Bob, who loves maps and travel, and has navigated our family through more than a few "Oh No!" moments.

Without you I would be lost.

Like for real lost - someone would have to come get me.

THE GRANDS GO... OH NO!

THE GRAND CANYON

Written By A.N. Eason

Illustrated by Toby Mikle

Text Copyright©2021 A.N. Eason
ISBN   978-1-7365753-4-5 paperback
ISBN   978-1-7365753-5-2 hardback
Library of Congress Control Number 2021913289

All rights reserved. This book may not be reproduced in whole or in part in any form, or by any means, without express written permission from the publisher.

Published by:
Reason Publishing
reasonprofessionals@gmail.com
Kingston, Tennessee

Illustrations by Toby Mikle

For information: www.grandsgo.com

*For Madelyn & Olivia —
Enjoy the Grand Canyon!
A. N. Eason
Romans 8:28*

This book belongs to:

_____

Three national parks are our destination;
This may be the best of all our vacations!

There is so much to do, but the list is in hand.

It ends with a day in a canyon that's Grand!

Then hiking a river should not be much trouble.

Next we'll see castles of rock stretching tall;

Zigzagging trails walk us up a red wall.

A lake we can boat in with water so blue,

That flows round a rock in the shape of a "U".

Driving all day, we arrive at the park,

Jumping out of the car just before dark.

We run to the rim, and the sun starts to sink,

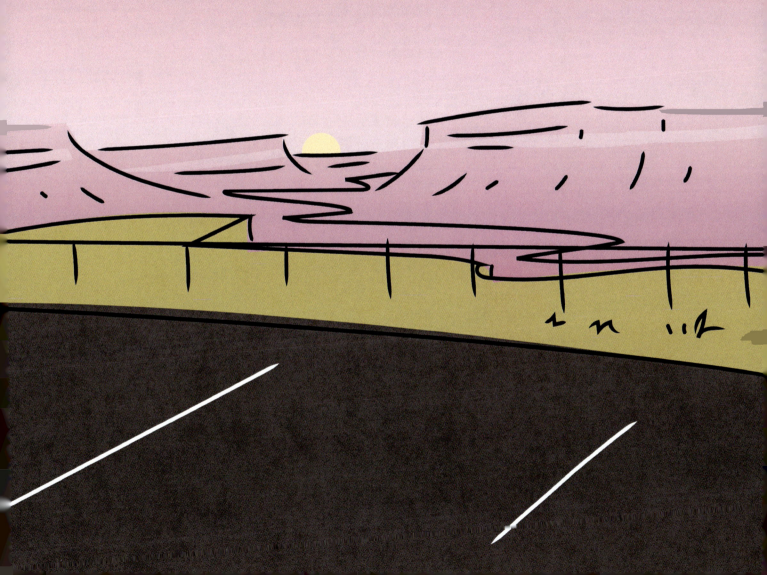

Watching in wonder as the sun fades from sight,

Sometimes you don't need hours or days;

That one perfect moment is the memory that stays.

And a detour can throw all their plans out of whack.

But we keep this in mind, this one thing we know,

Spending time with each other is the reason we go.

Trip Journal

Date _____

Who went

_____

_____

_____

Favorite Memory

_____

_____

_____

Scan to learn more about The Grands

There are 17 roadrunners in this book.

Did you find them all?

For Trip Suggestions, Playlists,
and more adventures with The Grands go to
www.grandsgo.com

Made in the USA
Middletown, DE
16 September 2021